Wanna Trade Families?

A PREACHER'S KID JOURNEY IN
SEARCH OF TRUTH, ACCEPTANCE,
AND WHOLENESS

Barbara Madaris Sullivan

TRILOGY CHRISTIAN PUBLISHERS
TUSTIN, CA

Trilogy Christian Publishers
A Wholly Owned Subsidiary of Trinity Broadcasting Network
2442 Michelle Drive
Tustin, CA 92780

For information, address Trilogy Christian Publishing

Rights Department, 2442 Michelle Drive, Tustin, Ca 92780.

Trilogy Christian Publishing/ TBN and colophon are trademarks of Trinity Broadcasting Network.

For information about special discounts for bulk purchases, please contact Trilogy Christian Publishing.

Manufactured in the United States of America

Trilogy Disclaimer: The views and content expressed in this book are those of the author and may not necessarily reflect the views and doctrine of Trilogy Christian Publishing or the Trinity Broadcasting Network.

10 9 8 7 6 5 4 3 2 1

Library of Congress Cataloging-in-Publication Data is available.

ISBN 978-1-63769-242-4

ISBN 978-1-63769-243-1 (ebook)

Contents

In memory of my cherished husband, Lee,
who shared and supported my deepest desire's
to be everything God created me to be.

1

Please Take My Problems

My dream for an ideal family would be one that is problem-free, with each member pulling off their mask revealing their true identity while loving each other unconditionally. If there is such a family, where have they been hiding? If you know of such a gem, please contact me. I want to trade. The truth is, no one has a free pass around problems; we do not like them, and they seem to follow us around regardless of where we are. We certainly don't look for them. We lie to ourselves if we believe we are the only ones to experience problems. They come in many different packages; some breaking our hearts while others give us headaches. It's not surprising to know we all have them, but silly to think ours are the worst.

There is an old African parable that goes like this:

Every morning in Africa, a gazelle wakes up. It knows it must run faster than the fastest lion, or it will be killed. Every morning a lion wakes up. It knows it must outrun the fastest gazelle, or it will starve to death. It doesn't matter if you are the gazelle or the lion. When the sun comes up, you better be running. They each have their own problem.

Each one learns from their problem. If the gazelle learns to run fast, he lives longer. If the lion learns to run fast, he eats. There's no hiding from the fact we each have our own problems also. It's not a bad thing to have problems because God uses our problems to teach us and develop our character. I have observed, through the years, it seems the only way to develop our character is by experiencing trouble.

I once read, has any man ever obtained inner harmony by simply reading about the experiences of others? Not since the world began has it ever happened. To understand the fire, each man must go through the fire himself. As a child, I did not believe my mother when she said, "do not touch the hot stove," until I felt the burning pain in my tiny finger.

In another story, all mankind stood before God and complained about their problems and trials forced upon them. They complained what they were going through was unfair, with everyone asking for relief.

God said, "put your problems on the table," and after they were placed, He told everyone, "go around and pick up someone else's problem to take back home." After carefully viewing the problems on the table, each one picked back up their own problem to deal with.

In my youth, I once heard someone say, "once we give our hearts to Jesus, we will never have any problems." While it is true Jesus has an answer to every problem, it is a deceiving statement to tell a new convert that once a Christian, you are immune from problems. Believing that lie will cause a new convert to give up on their faith, falling back into their sin at the first sign of trouble. Salvation does not shield us from problems but gives us the strength to walk through them. God's grace and mercy will help us not to jump ship in the middle of the storm.

> No temptation has overtaken you except such as is common to man; but God is faithful, who will not allow you to be tempted beyond what you are able, but with the temptation will also make the way of escape, that you may be able to bear it.
>
> 1 Corinthians 10:13

If God has the power to make a way of escape, why doesn't He just remove a Christian's problems altogether? For me, He turns the ugliness of my problems into good in order to develop my character, molding me more each day into His image.

There is no doubt we are living in a sin-cursed world. Our tenancies are to shift the blame for our problems to others most of the time, but too often, the results are from our own poor choices. Statistics say that 90 percent of our problems would disappear if we would do the right things.

How many family arguments would disappear if everyone at home were responsible and do what they should be doing?

For example: be on time for work, pick up after yourself, take out the trash, turn off the lights, clean the house, do your homework, be at home by your curfew. How much healthier would we be if we ate the right food? How much better would our finances be if we made a budget living within our means, stop coveting what others have, and pray for wisdom in our finances?

Wouldn't life be better if we learned from our mistakes, admitting we have problems instead of blame-shifting and making excuses for our behavior? Excuses are used to cover or hide the true reason behind our behavior. It is accomplished by either avoiding the truth or not telling the truth.

Have you heard that an excuse is worse and more terrible than a lie, for an excuse is a lie guarded? Too often, we run from our problems by making excuses. As I reflected back on my life, by not understanding my family's problems, I often made excuses for them. Of which I will talk about more later.

Problems are never planned and can come up quickly, as fast as a thunderstorm. There are warnings of the storm ahead to give us time to prepare, only too often we ignore those warnings. Prepared or not, we must ride out the storm.

Several years ago, on a trip to Columbia, Tennessee, to visit one of my spiritual sisters, as I approached Atlanta, it began to rain. The farther north I traveled, the worse it got. The clouded overcast was dark, and the rain was so hard I was barely able to see the car in front of me. My mom would have said it was "raining cats and dogs!" Only the emergency lights from the car in front kept me focused on the road and in my lane. Although I should have gotten a room for the night, I felt compelled to continue, driving slowly north toward Chattanooga. It seemed the Lord was gently pushing me on in the middle of this storm, my knuckles white as I gripped the steering wheel, shaking all the way.

Continuing on until I reached the other side of Chattanooga, I experienced something as never before driving up that mountain highway. The rain had ceased, but there were these beautiful waterfalls flowing over the cliffs on both sides of the road for miles; it was breathless and reminded me of God's beauty even after a bad storm. If I had pulled over the night before, I would have missed this amazing sight. By continuing my journey in the midst of the storm, the Lord showed me the end result of the storm, and it was spectacular.

My friend had been praying for me driving up and confused that God allowed me to fight such bad traffic and in a strong storm. I explained to her I was dealing with a spiritual storm in my life, and God was teaching me to persevere, to keep pushing forward no matter how dark it looked or how many tears I had cried even as I felt helpless and alone.

By trusting in Him as I rode out the physical storm, in the end, He revealed to me more of His majesty and beauty, ensuring me if I continued on in my spiritual storm, it would also be worth weathering the storm.

Nothing slips past the Father; there will be problems and storms. We will shed a lot of tears and experience heartaches in our journey. His help comes when we fully surrender to His purpose as we search for unanswered questions. As I focused on the car lights in front to guide me when my vision was bad, it was the lights that helped me stay in the middle of my lane.

We will weather the storms if we keep our focus on Jesus, for "He is the way, the truth, and the life" (John 14:6). Then Jesus spoke to them again, saying, "I am the light of the world. He who follows Me shall not walk in darkness, but have the light of life" (John 8:12). If we ride out the storm with our focus on Jesus, he will help us deal with our problems, and we will behold the beauty at the end of each one.

Regardless of how strong the rain and wind in every storm, I found safety in God as He covered me with His love of protection while developing my character. Through the years, I have ridden out many dark storms as I struggled with family problems while fighting the dark clouds hanging over my family; from those clouds many times impairing the truth and understanding of how to live a victorious life in Christ.

From my experience, I would not trade my problems and storms of life to pick up someone else's. By persevering through my own storms, even though I tried many times to hide in them, I learned not to hide from my problems. Doing so allowed God to change my character as He gave me more grace to overcome each one.

2

Dysfunctional to the Core

Many of my friends seem to have more childhood memories than myself, which has been frustrating as I listen to their cute little stories. Science reveals there is a lot more locked up in our memory than we recall. In our modern society, we have access to the internet where we can download our favorite music, movies or connect on social media, unlike the time I grew up in. With no internet or knowledge of a computer in my youth, we would grab the comic section of the weekend newspaper for our entertainment. I didn't understand a lot of the humor in those comics, but I loved looking at the colorful pictures.

One of my favorite cartoons was the "Family Circus." This syndicated comic strip was based on the life of Bill Keena, using the challenges and adventures of his suburban family. Recently, I ran across some of his work on-line to read that his son had continued with the cartoon after Bill's death. As times have changed, so have cartoons, especially in language. Today, our freedom of speech has become open and tainted than when I was young. My sister calls it a "potty mouth."

Regardless of the times, children still pick up on our words, good or bad, repeating what they hear and imitating what they see the adults do. Reading the cartoon in my days was funny because I could relate to some of the same scenarios happening in our family, as with the characters in the Family Circus. We are quick to laugh when we observed behavior in a dysfunctional family but experiencing it in your own family is somewhat painful.

There are many books written on the behavior described as being a "dysfunctional family," a term I never heard in my youth. It means not operating normally or properly. A dysfunctional family is one in which conflict, misbehavior, and often child neglect or abuse on the part of individual parents occur continuously and regularly, leading other members to accommodate such actions.

Below are some differences between a normal and not normal parent or family. My father fell into all ten descriptions of a not normal or dysfunctional parent.

Not Normal - dysfunctional	*Normal - functional*
1 - performance oriented	people oriented
2 - conformity demanded	diversity allowed
3 - dependent/ co-dependent	interdependent
4 - critical and judgmental environment	accepting and trusting environment
5 - inconsistent and legalistic rules	flexible rules
6 - many taboo subjects	all subjects open to discussion
7- protective of secrets	open and honest disclosure
8 - certain feelings unacceptable	all feelings acceptable
9 - punishment-shame & guilt enforcement	discipline & responsibility
10-unclear boundaries	clear boundaries

Of all the categories of abused children, the children of my family fell most into the Emotional/Psychological Abuse section. This form of child abuse and neglect includes acts or omissions by the parents or other person responsible for the child's care.

These acts may include:

- Habitual scapegoating, never accepting the responsibility of one's actions
- Belittling, lack of appreciation, very critical of everything
- Constantly treating siblings unequally regardless of reasons
- More concern with self rather than concern for the child's welfare

Emotional abuse can produce social disabilities that not only fail in many instances to improve with age but actually consume every area of the victim's life and relationships. While broken bones and bruises heal, the social lessons learned by those who are emotionally abused haunt the victim and pollute their relationships throughout their lifetime.

Another abuse we had to cope with was Spiritual Abuse. My father used his Bible in our home as a weapon. Other types of behavior he fell into were:

1. He displayed a distorted image of God, I believe, due to a godly father missing in his life.
2. He seemed more concerned with our spiritual performance demanding we be perfect but not applying the same spiritual principles to his life.

3. He had a distorted Christian image of himself because he never discovered who he could be in Christ.

4. There seemed to be a problem relating to the authority, which explained his lack of commitment.

5. He developed problems with personal boundaries in which he misused his power to invade others' boundaries.

6. His difficulty with personal responsibility revealed his focus more on others' sins, feeling they had a greater need for God than himself.

7. He had a hard time admitting any abuse in his family, so he would never admit his abuse. Shame keeps the abuse hidden.

8. He had a lack of trust in people saying often someone was always out to get him and he wasn't trustworthy himself.

He not only displayed this type of behavior but passed this abuse down to his children.

Children can grow up in such families with the understanding that such a situation is normal. Dysfunctional families are primarily a result of two adults, one typically overtly abusive, the other codependent, and may also be affected by addictions (substance abuse or sometimes mental illness). The parents may emulate or overcorrect from their own dysfunctional parent. In some cases, the dominant parent will abuse or neglect their children, and the other parent will not object, misleading a child to assume blamelessness at times to the third and fourth generations. Some refer to this as generational curses.

> You shall not bow down to them nor serve them. For I, the Lord your God, am a jealous God, visiting the iniquity (immoral or grossly behavior) of the fathers on the children to the third and fourth generations, of those who hate me.
>
> Exodus 20:5

> The Lord is longsuffering and abundant in mercy, forgiving iniquity and transgression; but He by no means clears the guilty, visiting the iniquity of the fathers on the children to the third and fourth generation.
>
> Numbers 14:18

> You shall not bow down to them nor serve them. For I, the Lord your God, am a jealous God, visiting the iniquity of the fathers on the children to the third and fourth generations of those who hate me.
>
> Deuteronomy 5:9

My journey to understand what happened to my Christian family was a hard, long, and discouraging time, always questioning God why mine was different in not measuring up to other families in the church.

Each family has its story, some are similar, and others are different. There is no escaping our sin-cursed world full of dysfunctional people and families. My parents are now deceased, but with permission and blessings from my siblings, they encouraged me to share my journey, praying others may learn, persevere and rise above the snares of a dysfunctional home.

3

Our Generational Consequences

If I were to write down my childhood memories, I could put them on one page until eight. My story will begin at that age, but first, I need to give you some background on my parents. My father had just left Lee College at age twenty-seven to attend Stamps Baxter's School of Music in Dallas, Texas, where he met my mother at the age of sixteen. After falling in love at first sight, they married shortly after.

Growing up in a small Georgia cotton mill town, my father had a call on his life to preach the Gospel very early in life, with his oldest brother already a minister. Being the youngest of seven children, he grew up without his father, losing him in death at the age of five. My grandmother never remarried. Working in the cotton mill, she struggled to raise her children the best she could. She was a godly little Pentecostal woman, only wore long dresses, no makeup, and her white hair grown down to her waist was pulled up in a bun. I only knew her with long white hair because she was in her late sixties when I was born. She was patient with us all, as rowdy as we were, cooking the best chicken and dumplings ever, and allowed us to spend many nights. I felt privileged to go to church with her and remember going to large tent revivals like Oral Roberts and others that came through the town.

My father was one of the most talented people I knew back in the day playing five different instruments; he had a good singing voice, very artistic in drawing, charismatic personality, with so many giftings that could have made him a very successful man if only he had applied them. He loved to visit different churches teaching voice lessons to the choir and preaching God's Word.

My mother was born in the Tennessee mountains but moved with her parents to Dallas, Texas, when she was fifteen. Hating the country, she felt like she was a bird let out of a mountain cage. She was young and naive for sure. Her father was an alcoholic, which led us to believe that was why my grandmother was so mean and not close to mom. Shortly after moving to Dallas, my mother got involved in church, giving her heart to Christ, the sad thing being her parents would not allow her to attend church. Instead of giving up her faith, she left home, moving in with her pastors.

That is where my parents met. My mother's love for God and music inspired her to sing like an angel. It was no surprise the two hooked up as a Christian couple with similar interests and talents. Their friends felt this was a marriage made in heaven. Their hopes for ministry and the future as a young couple were high.

She was pregnant with me when they moved back to Georgia, where my mother's nightmares began. The dreams and plans she had for ministry and family didn't turn out quite the way she had dreamed and prayed. Now she is living in a strange town, with only one friend, her mother-in-law. She was confused, feeling trapped from the horrific news she would receive in the days ahead. But one thing she was sure of, she deeply loved this talented, smooth-talking, good-looking man. She was overlooking his faults, doing as she was taught, to honor and obey, forgiving him every sin. Her downfall was believing every lie he told.

She became the codependent parent defined in the dysfunctional family, more often than she should, overlooking my father's actions as a husband and father. In her struggle to deal with horrific issues in the marriage, along with a lot of discouragement, she felt God had forsaken her as her dreams and visions of a balanced Christian family diminished. As her only coping mechanism, she secretly turned to alcohol and popped nerve pills to numb her pain. For years, she believed the

lies of the enemy as Satan whispered to her all her failures as a wife and mother. Her dreams of ministry had
been destroyed. Her anguish from the way he treated
her during their marriage was almost more than she
could bear. Now years later, this toxic relationship had
produced six children as his endless betrayal never
stopped, and she could not find a way out of this hell of
a marriage.

Her children not only lived with abuse, but she experienced emotional and sexual abuse. Undermining
a person's sense of self-worth by constant criticism,
belittling, silent treatments, subverting parent-child
relationships, making and breaking promises is char-
acteristic of emotional abuse.

Also, verbal assaults such as undermining a person's
sexuality by derogatory remarks, criticisms of desir-
ability, and unfounded accusations of infidelity consti-
tute abuse of a sexual nature. My mother would weigh
one hundred pounds, and he would not only make her
feel fat but also his girls. At eighty-five pounds, I was
wearing a girdle throughout high school, feeling I was
too fat. It was a miracle I didn't turn anorexic.

There were also unfounded accusations of infidelity, with him claiming all of us children to have had
different fathers, but all of that was just a screen to try
and hide his many years of infidelity. Even a fool could
see we all looked like him. Over time he had emotion-

ally beaten her down, damaged her self-image, causing her to fall deeper under his grips of power and control. Why did she stay thirty-one years in this relationship with such abuse hidden behind the name of Christianity? She had become afraid for herself, her children, trapped and manipulated.

And yes, my father was the very dominant, neglected, and abusive parent who drove church and religion down the throats of his children while he lived in the shadow of his hidden sins. Horrible stories began to unfold about her handsome, talented husband, where trust and faith in him began to deteriorate—beginning shortly after the move to her new town, finding out during childbirth with me that he had been locked up for statutory rape of a relative along with one of his brothers.

Keep in mind the scripture, "but He by no means clears the guilty, visiting the iniquity of the fathers on the children to the third and fourth generation" (Numbers 14:18).

The only way to know ourselves is to look deeply at our own lives on every level. What do we want from life? What do we think would make us happy? Everyone gambles his or her life on something or someone as the way to happiness. These were questions my parents had not asked themselves nor had found any answers. They did not realize themselves their view of happiness was distorted. You would think, them being in the church having a relationship with Christ, they had learned Jesus was the only one that could fill the void in their lives.

It was hard for me as a child to understand why we jump from one church to another. About the time I made friends and got involved, we were gone. I would hear them joke about being tagged as "church hoppers," not fully understanding the meaning for a long time. There were seasons we were very involved in the church; then we wouldn't go, confusing my little mind even more because I loved church and Sunday School. During some of those seasons, when my parents had strayed from their faith, the church was gracious enough to send a bus to take me. What an impact that had on my life. Without that bus ministry, my life would have turned out a lot different and not in a good way.

In my confusion and quest for answers, I began to hear about generational curses, as believed to be passed down from one generation to another due to rebellion against God. If your family is marked by divorce, incest, anger, or any other ungodly patterns, you're likely under a generational curse. These curses are tied to choices and can be broken.

We didn't have family gatherings like many other families that I was envying. I couldn't figure out why! There was only one family Christmas I remember at my grandmother's with all the aunts, uncles, and cousins. That was so much fun! When I was growing up, there were a couple of uncles we would visit periodically. They were always drunk, blowing money, cussing, causing my aunts to live in a daily hell. Some of their children were in trouble a lot, several spending time in jail. There was always drama in our circle. Very early after my exposure to that behavior, I vowed never to drink.

One Sunday, we traveled out of town to visit with my father's friends that were pastors. It was during one of those seasons that the family was not involved in a church. That night at the age of ten, I marched down to the altar to give my heart to the Lord, hoping they would follow. They did not that night, but I promised to follow Jesus and be an example, although very young. There was no playing church for me; I well heard the Holy Spirit call me to repentance. It was several months after, the night of my conversion, that my parents re-dedicated their hearts to Christ...again!

At that time, I had not begun playing the piano. I remember very young as my desire to do so increased; sitting on the front pew in the church, I would watch our pastor's wife play the huge, beautiful black grand piano as she led the choir. I never said this to anyone, but as a child, I would say to myself, "one day I will play that piano," and I did fifteen years later. Those that were my Sunday School teachers, pastors, and mentors will receive many jewels in their crowns, being instrumental in helping me become the woman of God that I am today. Because of their influence, they taught me the consequences of life.

There are consequences to our actions; God created us with free will. For every action, there is a reaction. Our human nature is to think we are in control of our lives, and like Adam and Eve, we try to hide our sins from God.

"But if you do not do so, then take note, you have sinned against the Lord; and be sure your sin will find you out" (Numbers 32:23). We fail to remember what we do in our lives may affect our children even to the third and fourth generation.

One of my brothers had gotten into trouble believing the consequences of his actions were only hurting him, but I had to remind him his actions had hurt the entire family. Thank God His grace and mercies are new each morning, breaking bondages from prior generations on our children and grandchildren.

There is the law of sowing and reaping. The fruit of our labor will always produce what we plant. You can't plant an apple seed to grow an orange tree. We can't plant diseased, rotten seeds in our spirit and expect healthy, productive consequences. While sin originated in the garden beginning with Adam and Eve, I believed somewhere in our family lineage, generational consequences were not dealt with. Rotten seeds were planted in the hearts of my family, resulting in unhealthy life-styles, but who planted them?

My Father knew the Bible well, but so does Satan. Just knowing the Word does not exempt you from the consequences of your sins and the sins of your father. Mine never could grab ahold of the truth that one day he would have to answer for the consequences of his actions.

First John 1:9 says, "if we confess our sins, He is faithful and just to forgive us our sins and to cleanse us from all unrighteousness."

4

A Sea of Questions

Shortly after my parents rededicated their lives back to Christ, things seemed to change, especially when we moved to Macon, Georgia. By now, I was twelve years old, growing stronger each day in my talents and relationship with God but still looking for answers, although not as much. My father was preaching again with a wonderful day job. Before then, I noticed he changed jobs as many times as churches, giving us believable excuses for the sudden change.

Mother was now able to be a stay-at-home mom. We were a lot happier with her there every afternoon when we came home from school than with a babysitter. Although we had to jump right on our homework, it was more of a pleasant experience than before, as we would smell the wonderful aromas of dinner cooking coming from the kitchen, anticipating playtime after dinner. The kids in our neighborhood would gather together to play a game of softball every afternoon. We lived in a great community with many friends and continued to be very active in our church.

The three siblings after me, one brother and two sisters, were now in first, second, and third grades. Growing more in my ability to play the piano, my brother learned to play the drums as I sang with my two sisters and sometimes with my parents. The two years in Macon were the most memorable times of our childhood that soon ended, only to move back to our hometown.

Unfortunately, one of my aunts had a mental breakdown and was found hiding under the bed dressed with multiple layers of clothes, begging to "not let them get her." Not let "who" get her? was my question. With no answer, I could only speculate. Because my aunt had to go to a mental hospital, my grandmother had to give up housekeeping. She wanted to move in with us, but only if we move back to our home town. Move back? Please, God, no! My mother and I cried for two weeks when we got the news.

Not fully understanding why it was hard living back in our hometown, I kept searching for answers while my list for God kept growing. The adults certainly wouldn't tell me anything, only to ignore me when I questioned them. Something was not right as I sensed a heavy dark cloud hanging over our family become more of a mystery. Like Moses wandering in the wilderness, I felt like I had been wandering around in a desert until we moved to Macon for those two years, only to start wandering again. Something had a hold on my parents living in that town, which could very well be Generational Curses. My questions continued; will we stop attending church as a family again? Will my father not work again?

Feeling guilty questioning God a lot, I learned I was not the only one with a lot of questions after reading David's many questions as he searched for answers.

> How long O' Lord? Will You forget me forever? How long will You hide Your face from me? How long shall I take counsel in my soul, having sorrow in my heart daily? How long will my enemy be exalted over me? Consider and hear me, O Lord my God; Enlighten my eyes lest I sleep the sleep of death; lest my enemy say I have prevailed against him. Lest those who trouble me rejoice when I am moved. But I have trusted in Your mercy; My heart shall rejoice in Your salvation. I will sing to the Lord, Because He has dealt bountifully with me.
>
> Psalm 13:1-6

That was how I felt in my youth! I knew God heard me but felt He, along with my family, kept hiding answers from me. How long, Lord, how long?

In my quest for answers and lack of understanding, I held on to "honor your father and mother, that your days may be long upon the land which the Lord Your God is giving you." Exodus 20:12 and also Ephesians 6:1-4 say:

1. "Children, obey your parents in the Lord, for this is right.
2. Honor your father and mother, "which is the first commandment with promise;
3. that it may be well with you and you may live long on the earth.
4. And you, fathers, do not provoke your children to wrath, but bring them up in the training and admonition of the Lord."

During my wilderness journey, even in the middle of my confusion, I kept honoring them as my parents, although my questions continued to grow with no answers in sight.

How did my grandfather die? Why were so many of my father's siblings alcoholics when they were raised by a godly mother? Why did my family struggle with their commitment to God? Why did I always have this feeling that people seemed to look down on us? I sensed the gossip and rejection from the church, but why?

Why wasn't my father able to hold down a job very long? Why was his family at odds all the time? Why did so many pastors turn him down for revivals? Why was he so controlling? Why was he so negative? Regardless of what we did, why couldn't He compliment and encourage all of us? Why, why, why?

In comparing my family to others in the church, I continued to question God, "Why can't we be like them?" But regardless of my why's, I tried to honor them both.

5

Hidden Sins

All hell broke loose as soon as we moved back to our hometown. Looking back on what I thought was a peaceful family season in life, something cynical had to be going on in my father's heart before the move, like the same repeated behavior played out soon after my parents move from Dallas. Sin never accidentally or suddenly happens. Our sins are borne first in our hearts, and then they are acted on.

> But those things which proceed out of the mouth come from the heart, and they defile a man. For out of the heart proceed evil thoughts, murders, adulteries, fornications, thefts, false witness, blasphemies.
>
> Matthew 15:18-19

The heart is deceitful above all things, and desperately wicked; Who can know it? I, the Lord, search the heart. I test the mind, even

to give every man according to his ways, and
according to the fruit of his doings.

Jeremiah 17:9-10

It was August, a few months before my fourteenth
birthday. My brother, father, and I packed up and drove
our first load of furniture back to our hometown while
mom stayed in Macon with my sisters. It was fairly late,
so we spent the night after unloading the truck. That
night my view of my father was shattered. The protection and safety I once felt as a little girl was now gone.

There is no need to share in detail the actions of
my father, but in his attempt to seduce me, God's pro-
tective hand of mercy stopped it. Pray continually for
protection over your children. I experienced firsthand
God's mercy from the many prayers I heard prayed for
me as a child. Even though his intentions were stopped
that night, years later, as he continued to play out his
fantasies, the court still considered his attempt against
me as "child molestation."

Day after day, I was haunted by the question, "what
did I do to cause this attempt?" I was young and naive
at the time, but I knew this was not healthy and certainly not becoming as a Christian father. The family
list of questions had grown with no answers, only now
to deal with a secret of my own, a secret that became
a heavy cross to bear for a teenager. Do I dare tell my

mom, knowing it could destroy what I thought was a wonderful Christian father, or remain silent? So silent I remained, becoming more tormented than ever as I searched for answers.

Before then, I was so excited at church to stand and testify of my thankfulness for a Christian family, only now to have that image perverted. Thinking back on those days, I wondered how many people knew answers to my family secrets, only to wonder even more if they were feeling sorry for my ignorance.

The next month I started the eighth grade gaining some clarity on why my family seemed to have such a stigma on our last name. On my first day, a teacher made the remark, "Oh no, another one," repeating my maiden name. She was comparing me to previous relatives she had taught. I was immediately put in the same box as them, being judged with the same bad, rebellious reputation.

It was heartbreaking as a teen dealing with a different kind of peer pressure. My thoughts were, *I am a Christian; how can you compare me to them when you do not know me? I am not like them.* From that day forward, her comment sent me on a quest to prove to the town, the churches, and my teachers that I was different, a quest that continued most of my life.

Dealing with my family stigma along with my secret pushed me into a deep depression as a teenager. It became a hard, dark burden to carry as I begin to question my own self-worth. My heart became heavy for those who had experienced much worse abuse than I.

My struggle increased more each day, dealing with the guilt of "what happened" even to what "could have happened" until the pain was unbearable, giving me suicidal thoughts. There can be no healing when we keep things bottled up in our souls. The dark things in our lives cannot be dealt with until they are exposed to the light.

One dark, cold winter night, I decided to stop my pain and confusion as I sat up in bed, swinging my feet to the floor to pause a minute before opening the bedroom door. My plan was to get a kitchen knife then put an end to all my pain and questions. I loved my father and knew by exposing him, the consequences would be bad, not only destroying my mother but the family as I knew it. But the fear of being alone with him with the "what if it happened again, or going even further" was becoming more than I could bear.

As I approached my door, I felt the Holy Spirit overshadow me as though freezing me in place while He softly whispered of how much He loved me; ensuring me what happened was not my fault; to not feel guilty; assuring me, He would never leave me. Weeping, I fell on my knees next to my bed, asking the Lord to forgive me for what I was about to do, also forgiving my father.

Jesus saved my life again. That burden became less heavy when I eventually shared my story with a trusted friend but still remained silent with my mother. My father never mentioned to me the events of what happened that night as he continued to preach some, even pastoring a couple of churches.

It was only by God's mercy and grace that I was able to march forward with my life. My mother had my little brother and another one two years later, bringing the number of children to six, with me being the oldest. My brothers and sisters are now older and more rebellious as the days go by. I felt rebellion too but was the compliant child, quiet, but questioning, *why can't they be like me?* The atmosphere in our home was bad, full of drama.

All of us kids continued to sing and play. The older they got, the more challenging it became trying to minister in music with them. By this time, they were in their early teens, growing more defiant each passing year. I was finished with school, working, and still living at home. The more he crammed church down our throats, the more rebellious they became and the more secluded I became. As teens, we all dealt with some rebellion being part of growing up trying to establish our own identity. What I didn't know until years later was theirs were magnified because they had seen him do evil acts, finding out about his secret sins, of which

I was still in the dark. How, after all this time, could I have been so naive and unknowledgeable? For whatever reason, it was like God put me into this safety bubble that hid parts of his life from me for a season.

The more my brothers and sisters matured, the more rebellious they became. My mother lovingly spanked us, and to this day, we still laugh about those little peach tree switches. But my father would beat us in anger with the nearest object he could grab; broom, coat hanger, it didn't matter. The beatings and screams I was hearing from my siblings were becoming more unbearable each day. We often heard him say, "If I can't control my own household, how can I manage a church?" I guess he felt our rebellion was going to embarrass and ruin his name, the truth being he had already polluted his name. He had a spirit of control. All of us were in a battle fighting for our own identity.

My daily life was centered around the church and my job. When at home, I hid in my room sewing until I was so tired and numb that I could fall asleep. While some of the family coped with life using drugs and alcohol, I became a workaholic striving more each year to perfect my performance mode. That was my only way to survive in our daily family drama. The more my list of questions grew, the more I alienated myself from everyone as I coveted other Christian families. Dreams of singing and playing together as a happy family increased while following other talented families that ministered together. My desire for a close relationship with my siblings ran deep, but I remained alone and rejected, believing it was because of my faith.

Children should be able to grow up with a father that loves them unconditionally. We did not have that. All we had was fear, control, and alienation. My view of God, my heavenly Father, was distorted with the same attributes. It seemed the only time I got attention from my earthly father was when I was playing music. We all had to work for his recognition, craving approval as we developed the same mindset toward God. I believed the more I worked for God's Kingdom, the more He would love me. My workaholic addiction pushed me into several burnouts from working myself to death in the church, looking for approval and recognition not only from my father but my peers and God.

It wasn't long before my father fell back into his same pattern of defeat; again backslidden, washed up in ministry, and no job. My mother, by this time, had grown stronger in Christ, gaining the determination of a bulldog to remain faithful to God and her calling. She had gone through so much heartache with him she no longer believed his lies. The more she grew in Christ, the less dependent she became of him. God had restored her wasted years, her joy, and her new self-worth of being His daughter. She was no longer co-dependent but blossomed more into the beautiful woman God had called her to be all along.

6

Answers Accompanied by Tears

Even though I was afraid of my father and hiding my own secret, I continued to search out those unspoken secrets in our family. There was no hate in my heart, for I had forgiven him the night I wanted to end my life. I loved and honored him, although I disagreed with him on most issues. There was one opinion in our home, and it was his. You didn't dare give yours.

The closer my relationship with Christ blossomed, the more distant I became in my relationship with my brothers and sisters. Being mocked, accused of being a goody-two-shoes, and selfish was making my life harder. How was I selfish when I made their clothes, worked to help feed them, buying Christmas gifts several years when our parents could not afford to? But I would tell myself, "Don't complain." After all, Christ had to endure more than I could ever comprehend. Regardless, the more I did for them, the more unthankful they became. The more I did, the more used I felt. Some of the cruelest persecutions can come from your family, the ones you love the most.

More focused on my petty issues with them than what was happening in their lives, my father continued beating them for hardly anything and verbally abusing them. One incident was so bad with screams I had to step in to stop the beating. In his opinion, we couldn't do anything right. He believed his actions were justified because they were defying him with a lack of respect. I guess he thought he would beat Jesus into them. Because I had not gotten any spankings since twelve, I could understand why my siblings felt there was favoritism.

Eventually, we all got married, moving out of that house as soon as we could. My siblings were close to each other, but as usual, I felt unwanted and unwelcomed as a family member. I finally convinced myself it was because of my faith and their lack of. My mother continued to be very active in the church while my father fell back into the same old pattern, one he had known for most of his life.

Be careful what you pray for. God hears our prayers but the answers are not always one you would want to have a victory dance over. When the answers to my questions begin to come, it was like a fast-moving, cold waterfall. My heart was so grieved I thought I would drown from my tears. Now a young woman myself at age thirty, my mother unveiled all the secrets that haunted me, and it was more than I could barely handle. I prayed many years for the truth to be revealed but never thought I would get it all at one time. That day the answers I received were accompanied by many tears continuing for weeks ahead. She hid them from me for a long time because she didn't want me to lose my respect for him. Little did she know, I had lost that a long time ago!

After thirty-one years of marriage, she could not deal with him anymore. She had forgiven him until there was no more forgiveness in her heart. She was tired of the lies, excuses, the cheating, and verbal abuse she and her children had endured all this time.

The more she shared, the more shocked I became. It was then I learned he was in jail for statutory rape when I was born. What a frightening experience for her to give birth to her first child alone, as what she thought in the beginning was her hero, sitting in a jail cell for statutory rape? How could this happen a few months in Georgia after being so involved in ministry back in Texas a few months prior? She didn't have to tell me about his porn addiction; I already knew his struggle with that demon because as a child, I would find his porn magazines while searching for hidden Christmas presents. She shared that a lot of incest in his family had occurred through the years by more than one sibling, hidden by family members.

She continued sharing how multiple affairs had occurred with many women she thought were her friends and with more than she probably knew. He also tried to seduce one of my sisters, but unlike me, she told mom; but once again, he convinced mother it was a lie, that my sister was just rebellious and out to get him. It was then I told her my secret, regretting I had been quiet for so long, thinking if I had told, it might have spared my sister from her experience.

What brought this toxic relationship finally to a halt was my father, who was pastoring again, with only my mother working. He was having an affair with the young lady across the street. She was the same age as my baby sister with five children and was also a member of the church. Two weeks before my mother exposed him later to file for a divorce, he resigned one Sunday morning, giving us no reason as he walked out. Without knowing anything at this point, I broke down and sobbed. It was a strange feeling, like one of death. It was as if the father I thought I knew had just died.

Later as I relived that conversation, I couldn't help but think about all his talents, education, and how he had allowed Satan to ruin his life. Even with his knowledge of God's Word, he was not able to deal with all his sin issues. As the secrets were revealed more to me in the days ahead, I realized his life had been played with a generational curse that he did not recognize. He refused to see that Satan was destroying not only his life but the lives of his family. If he had only repented, kept the faith striving to be a Godly husband and father, who knows what he could have done for Christ. Curses would have been broken over our family.

Not long after my parents divorced, he married the young lady with five small children. Did he learn anything or repent? No, he got much worse! The wages of sin are death. He continued to spiral down a road of no return, continuing to find excuses and justifying his actions.

7

A Father's Love

You would think as the dark secrets of my family begin to unfold, my curiosity would have subsided. Over the next few years, I read every Christian self-help book I could find to receive some closure of my father's actions, still yearning for a different family, one I could be proud of.

Understanding from God's Word how Satan operates to kill and destroy lives, I realized my father's addictions had to start at an early age. Each time he appeared to get rid of an addiction, in his weakness from not repenting, he would fall back into bondage. Each time he reopened those doors, he allowed more demons to enter his spirit, reaching a point in his life that he believed he was doing nothing wrong. Who, in his life, influenced such hideous behavior? Whose life was he watching? Something evil had happened in our ancestry lineage.

Not a lot of information about my grandfather was available. I was told from the family he was a farmer who died in his early forties from a sickness that remained unknown to me. One of my aunts would often giggle as she whispered that my grandparents were cousins. In my research in our ancestry census records, I found they were, in fact, second cousins, with their parents being first cousins. With most of my family deceased, I may never know their history.

One statement my father made repeatedly every time something went wrong in his life, "He never had a chance in life because he was raised by a poor widow woman." He said it when he lost a job when church people shunned him, refusing revivals, using that as his biggest excuse for his sinful actions. He was always looking for a scapegoat.

Scapegoats were mentioned in Exodus and Leviticus to be part of a ceremony on the Day of Atonement. It was an animal ritual where the goat would be burden down with the sins of others and then driven away from the community. This act was an atonement for their sins. Our flawed human nature is we have a tendency when, making mistakes instead of accepting our failure to learn from them, we try to attach that fault to others. We put our mistakes or our sins on a goat and send him away. While some can be unfairly blamed, my father could only blame himself for his choices which he refused to do. Each sin he committed, he put it on the back of someone else, never accepting the consequences of his own sins.

He lost his dad at the age of five, with older brothers being the only male influence in his life, and from what I encountered, they were not good ones. I can only speculate what he learned from them was drinking, running around, incest, adultery, and playing with God. My godly grandmother had to endure a lot of hell dealing with her children with her mistakes of trying to conceal their behavior. Mothers want to protect their children, but they must hold them accountable for their actions. Instead of accountability, it was apparent that my grandmother enabled them, then tried to hide their sins.

I wondered how different my father's life might have turned out if he had grown up with a father or a strong Christian male mentor. His life could have gone an entirely different direction. But it's not always in the way you were raised that determines your outcome and success in life. Our will exercises the power of choice. He made too many bad choices.

The book of 1 Samuel reveals to us the story of the Prophet Samuel. His dad was Elkanah, and his mother, Hannah. We know that Hannah was the second wife of Elkanah and unable to have children. After her many prayers, God answered, giving her a son whom she named Samuel. She kept her vow to God, leaving him at the temple once weaned for the service of the Lord.

From a glimpse into the life of his father, Elkanah, his name means "God as created" or "God had taken possession." He was a son of Jeroham from the tribe of Levi. Elkanah deeply loved Hannah giving her double portions of blessings; he seemed to be a kind man, faithful to the Lord with a willingness to allow his little son to leave home to live in the house of the Lord. That in itself was a demonstration of deep trust in God.

We are not told how Samuel might have felt growing up without his father and mother, only to see them once a year when they returned to the city for yearly sacrifices. As Samuel grew, each year, his mother would bring him a new robe she had made, one for him to minister in. Children being children, as you know, have many questions rolling around in their little minds as they grow up; and no doubt he had his. Can you imagine only seeing your parents once a year?

Many of his questions may not have been answered, especially while watching Eli's family drama day after day unfold around the temple. One thing we do find special in the Word: "And the child Samuel grew in stature and in favor both with the Lord and with men" (1 Samuel 2:26).

Life can feel unfair sometimes when you are striving to learn and be obedient to God, often lonely. Did he feel pushed to the side as Eli allowed his sons to do their own thing? It had to be hard for him to watch the wickedness as the sons of Eli defiled the outside of the temple having sex with the women at the door, as he refused to participate. Even when the sons took the best of the sacrifices for themselves, Samuel made different choices. Eli may have taught Samuel God's Word, but he failed by example to obey God's commandments as he continued to condone the sins of his sons. It's one thing to know God's Word, but another to actually live it. By Samuel making the right choices, he found favor with people and with God.

While my father was very knowledgeable in God's Word, he only applied the scripture of his choosing. Like Levi's sons that took what they wanted without any repentance, he did the same. My father never learned that redemption comes when we recognize the root of our problem begins in our hearts. As we apply God's Word and power to our lives, repent, walk in obedience to God, only then will the chains of bondage be broken.

Like me, perhaps Samuel questioned Eli's character as he struggled with Eli allowing his children to commit unimaginable sins in and around the temple. That was one problem my precious grandmother dealt with. It was apparent she hid the sins of her children that progressed worse each year, enabling them to continue in their foolishness. I believe their lives would have been different if those sins had been exposed early on. Even if she was ashamed and perhaps wishing she was in a different family, her lack of action tarnished not only the character of the children but hers as well. Our hidden sins must be exposed in order to deal with them regardless of how ugly they are. We may hide our actions from people for a while, but all-seeing God doesn't miss a thing.

Year after year, Samuel continued his devotion and faithfulness to his God, not participating in the sins of Eli's family. Because of his choices, he grew in character and favor with God and other men. In comparing my father growing up to that of a young Samuel, they each did not have their fathers around daily as a mentor. One thing Samuel did do in the middle of his chaos, he stayed focus on God being faithful to his calling whether Eli dealt with his Sons or not. My father knew God's Word too! They each had a choice. Samuel chose to follow God's heart, where my father chose to follow his own.

My family did not experience a true father's love. How could he be a loving father when he had not experienced one himself?

The role model we had was perverted, for he was very self-centered, controlling, and competitive. Us kids felt all he wanted from us was to make him look good in the community. With music being one of his passions,

I felt the only way to gain his love and recognition was to advance in my music abilities, but that turned into a nightmare because he was so competitive.

I read that this type of father was abandoned by his own father, prompting him to overcompensate in his attempts to be manly. I suppose my grandfather dying when he was five could have triggered some type of abandonment feelings. It is said that the male identity is quite fragile and must be protected at all costs, even from his own children. This often shows up in the way he plays with them: There must always be a winner and a loser, and the winner must always be dad.

It also added that the daughters of competitive fathers often feel the contempt that these fathers seem to have for women. Even though the father may try to behave appropriately toward women, there is an undercurrent of hidden hostility that eventually comes through. Some therapists believe that this hostility is centered on the man's own mother; at a deep, unconscious level, he blames her for his father's leaving, even though he is not aware of these feelings. Denial becomes a way of life, not only for the competitive father but also for everyone else in the family.

By my father's competitiveness in his subconscious, could it be that he had some underlying hostility toward his mother for his dad not being in his life even though he had died, or because she never remarried? I come to this conclusion because of the statement we often heard when things went wrong for him; "He didn't have a chance in life because his mother was a poor widow woman." It sounds to me like he always blamed her for not having a male in her life and being poor. Maybe he would have turned out differently if he had grown up with his father.

That competitiveness was hard for us children. The more I advanced past him in my music and my career, the more critical and jealous he became of what I had accomplished. And as for love, only once in my lifetime did he say, "I love you."

Most people don't think about God as our model for fatherhood. My view of God was distorted in the way I viewed God to be more like my father, rather than my father like God.

I found there are several basic roles of fathering;

- He is loving, tender, gracious toward his children
- He lays out the rules, sets out the example, makes it possible to live by
- He fights for us, protects us from our enemies
- He teaches us revealing who God is through Jesus being a Spiritual mentor

Although I worshipped and lived for God as my creator, my view of Him based on my father's example was one of a harsh relationship, demanding of His people and always expecting too much. Believing these lies, I continued in my performance mode, working long and hard to try to gain more love from God.

Three years after my parents' divorce, God gave my family a miracle, one of the greatest gifts (other than salvation), our stepdad. For the rest of this story, you will know him as my dad, John.

This retired Navy man from a Pentecostal family was very much aware upfront he was marrying into a dysfunctional family with many wounds but chose to be part of our family anyway. I told mom that God not only gave this loving, Christian man to be her husband, but He also gave us children a Godly example of a father's love. Now I was getting closer to the family I had long for most of my life. Over the next twenty-five years, before the Lord took him home, he was my hero. He was not perfect by any means and didn't try to be, but he taught me the true meaning of a father's love.

From his example of a loving father, I began a new season of learning who my Heavenly Father was as my dad mentored me, forgiving me many times for my shortcomings with a non-judgmental attitude, loving me unconditionally. I had read and heard of God's unconditional love, but it wasn't until then that I grabbed ahold of the meaning of God's love for me. My dad's love revealed to me how much God wanted a relationship, not performance. Until then, I had been working myself to death, thinking the more I did for Him, the more He would love me. I had believed a lie from hell.

8

Honor Thy Fathers

It was heartbreaking, and I felt hopeless as I watched my family follow the same paths of generational curses as those that lived before, also hiding behind their sins. My only source of survival was to dive into the Bible.

Of all the people God gave us in His Word, I have related to King David the most; a man after God's own heart. Because of God's calling on my life as a musician and worship leader, over time, I found myself looking more deeply into David's life for direction and wisdom. My desire was to be "a woman after God's heart."

Remember the days when our Sunday School teacher taught us Biblical lessons on the felt boards? I can still visualize the figures of little David as a shepherd boy, expressing his love as he protected the little sheep, quick to kill anything, bear, or lion that sought to endanger the flock. The most popular among those displays were of David and Goliath, being one of the most inspiring stories burned deep into the pages of my childhood memory.

In the Word, I followed David's life as a musician and worship leader, observing the joys and heartaches he encountered on his personal journey. One story picks up after David has slain Goliath, where King Saul and David's relationship had grown to a deeper level. David loved his King dearly, often addressing him as his father. First Samuel 24:11 says, "moreover, my father, see! Yes, see the corner of your robe in my hand!" He desired a deep relationship with Saul, recognizing he was God's anointed. Saul became jealous of David's popularity that sparked his desire to kill him. Even though God withdrew His anointing on Saul, David stilled honored him as being anointed of God. David's love for Saul, whom he often called "father," was not tainted, although Saul tried countless times to kill him.

The more David ran and hid for his life, the more love and mercy for Saul thrived. He refused to kill him and would not allow others to hurt his King. In 2 Samuel, David, along with his men, had to hide out in Philistine from Saul, although they were still one of Israel's greatest enemies. God had given David favor with the King of Philistine, with the King recognizing his kingdom was being blessed as long as he protected David. The nation of Philistine embarked on another attack on King Saul, but when some of the warlords saw David as part of the army, they forbid him to engage in battle for fear David and his men would turn against them. I see God's mercy on David in sparing him from going to battle with his people. God will spare us heartache and pain if we are obedient to His calling. We should not go to war with our families.

All during King David's reign after Saul died, as long as he was obedient to the Lord, the nation enjoyed God's blessings, but when David was disobedient, the nation suffered hardship. God will always bless the family when the family head follows His guidelines in that family but will be cursed and suffer hardship when the head is walking in disobedience.

There was a constant division between Saul and David's household. Saul not only tried to take David's life repeatedly, but he gave His daughter in marriage, David's wife, to another man; he also delayed David's position as King as long as he could. Saul tried to destroy his honor, trust, home, and influence, but worst of all, he tried to destroy his relationship with Jonathan, David's most loved friend.

Yet David continued to honor Saul even after death in executing several men that tried to take credit for Saul's death, and he made sure Johnathan's son was taken care of for life.

In this example of David and his relationship with Saul, how can I deny the honor I must have for my father? There were many similarities between Saul and my father. They both were anointed at one time. They both were handsome in statue, talented, and started out life with a purpose. Both turned away from God and opened doors to demonic activity in their lives. Both lied to their families and tried to kill the spirits of their children.

Even in my youth, dealing with every issue I faced with him, I repeatedly kept in my heart, "honor your father and your mother, as the Lord your God has commanded you, that your days may be long and that it may be well with you in the land which the Lord your God is giving you" (Deuteronomy 5:16).

It was a constant challenge, but I believed God's promise I would live long if I did. I silently disagreed with them on most issues but honored, obeyed, and respected them more *for who they were*, being my parents and not so much as to *what they did with their lives*.

I never stopped loving my father in all of his shortcomings of life. Because of his unwillingness to change his life, he was sentenced to life in prison, where he died at the age of ninety-two. As far as I know, none of us ever received an apology from him or an admission of his sins. I am confident from conversations with the warden that he repented making things right with God. It has been a sad journey for our family but a learning one as we watched how disobedience to God, believing lies of the devil and how poor choices can ruin one's life.

As David honored Saul, I must still honor and love him for being my father, repeating "it's not in how he lived but who he was in my life." As I heard a friend say one time, "it's not how you started, but how you finished." I believe I will soon see him again, finally changed and whole.

9

Fighting for Recognition

We've all heard the saying, "being the oldest child is the hardest with the youngest, having it the easiest." I was four years old before my brother, and two sisters came along like doorsteps a year between each. My mom had a brother after our move back home and another brother when I was in high school. For me, that old saying was true; my parents were the hardest on me, but for my baby brother, it seemed he became more neglected than spoiled, in the sense that my parents were so caught up in their own issues of life not realizing he had demons of his own to fight.

I always felt like there were three sets of kids, at times with me being just another parent. It was hard hearing them say they were practicing parenthood on me. Where's the fun in an experiment? But my siblings never saw it that way. They often accused me as the favorite or the pet. What they didn't realize at the time was the age difference; I had gained my parents' trust because I had given my life to Christ at an early age, striving hard at being good, desiring their approval. That is when my "people pleaser skills" developed. It drove a wedge between us, and we were never close growing up. I went to work at seventeen to help mom provide for them being my father unemployed again. The more I tried to help them, the more rejected I felt. The more rejected I became, the more I longed to be part of another family, always comparing them to other church families.

My fight for recognition didn't actually start until I was in the eighth grade after moving back to my hometown starting with a teacher's comment from their dealings with the past family. I was bound and determined to be different in every way. I became obsessed with what others thought of me.

When not in school, church, or work, I was locked up in my room, sewing, making clothes for my mom, myself, and sisters, who carried over to the church family as my skills advanced. Being lost in my own little world was my only outlet distancing me more in my relationship with my siblings.

The more engaged in my battle for recognition, the more alienated I became. My years at home while singing and playing with my siblings often felt like David dodging Saul's spear each time he played. They wanted no part, and it was a battle each time our father made us sing together. The harder the battle, the more ashamed I became.

My greatest fight for recognition was with my father. His passion for music pushed me over and above my limits many times. I longed for compliments from him as I played and sang, hoping to please him each time. There were no compliments for any of us, only criticism when we did wrong. Our taste in music was so different; mine was moving more toward praise and worship vs. southern gospel and hymns. Too often, I had to sneak around to play or listen to my favorites, careful to never express my desires for change. Because he was competitive and controlling, it was his way or no way.

Through the years, I grew musically, not only playing but directing several different church choirs, singing groups, and bands. God blessed me beyond words in the ministry of music that He had anointed me for. But the more God gave me favor with the church and the people, the stronger my performance mode grew, becoming more concerned with the opinions of people. As I ran and hid from issues in my home, my strongholds grew.

It was years down the road before I learned "recognition" had become a spiritual stronghold in my life. It carried over into my career also. I was asked in an interview one time, "what was my greatest weakness?" I said, "I'm a people-pleaser." The interviewer said he liked people-pleasers, and I believe I got the job from that one statement. This kind of attitude is not only in the business world but has crept into the church. Most pastors want laymen on staff that beckon at their every call. You really find the motive of a pastor's heart when you disagree with him, especially verbally.

Unlike my father's strongholds, I was not immune from my own. My issues had turned into bitter envy of wanting another family and self-seeking recognition. My questions to find out the secrets of my family turned into more about lifting me up because, after all, I was the good kid.

Who is wise and understanding among you? Let him show by good conduct that his works are done in the meekness of wisdom. But if you have bitter envy and self-seeking in your hearts, do not boast and lie against the truth. This wisdom does not descend from above, but is earthly, sensual, demonic. For where envy and self-seeking exist, confusion and every evil thing are there. But the wisdom that is from above is first pure, then peaceable, gentle, willing to yield, full of mercy and good fruits, without partiality and without hypocrisy. Now the fruit of righteousness is sown in peace by those who make peace.

James 3:13-18

Each of us has a hard time seeing our own faults, failures, and sins. The more I pray and write, the more ugliness I see in my own life. No arguments here, for we were all born in sin, knowing we all have sinned, but we can't use that for an excuse to not deal with our heart sins. I hate when I hear people say, "we are just sinners saved by grace," which, most of the time it's an excuse to continue in their own sins. Yes, we were lost before getting saved, but once we are saved, we become righteous before God and covered by the blood of the Lamb. People that have known me for years will say I have good conduct and reputation, but now I see my works were not so much out of meekness, wisdom, and purity, more like self-seeking and envy. Only God sees the depths of the heart.

I have to admit my quest for a different family may have started innocent but over time turned into bitter envy of others and self-seeking. It was a hard word from James when he said, "envy and self-seeking exist, confusion and every evil thinking will be there." Ouch—I had been very careful not to envy material things from others but not recognizing envy of family's, relationships, and self-comparison fall under the same category. Strongholds were much darker in my life than I had imagined.

My healing with God was a slow process as I allowed Him to pull back layer after layer of my damaged heart. There are times when God heals instantly while others will be a process. The more I prayed that my spiritual eyes are open and for wisdom, the more my heart was revealed, and it wasn't pretty. Over time I became more gentle, more peaceable, giving more mercy, becoming more of a God-pleaser than a people-pleaser. I began to walk out of the darkness that plagued me for a long time into the light.

Out of the Darkness into the Light

Most Monday mornings roll around fast, and this was one of those Mondays. I started walking extra early with only the crickets and frogs making soft melodies way before the crack of dawn. The birds were asleep with the rabbits still snuggled in their dens. Most of the neighborhood streets are well lit with light poles and front porch lights except for one small section where the neighbors decided it wasn't worth spending money for outside lights.

About the time I reached that particular section, my fourth time around the block, I noticed a cat about to cross the street until he caught my silhouette in the dark as I marched down the middle of the street. In fear, he froze for a second then scurried to the other side, hiding under a car in the dark. Because of the darkness, he thought I didn't see him. He felt safe in the dark hiding under the car, not realizing it could be a death trap for him if the driver were to back up over him.

It is sinful nature in our hearts to try to hide anything in our personal darkness thinking no one can see just how dark our hearts really are. The Word reads:

> The heart is deceitful above all *things*, and desperately wicked; who can know it? I, the LORD, search the heart, *I* test the mind, even to give every man according to his ways, according to the fruit of his doings.
>
> Jeremiah 17:9-10

We read in the beginning, Adam and Eve tried to hide behind leaves in the garden after their disobedience. They found out pretty quickly that God knew exactly where they were and what they did.

My best analogy to compare our hearts/minds is to use computers as an example. Keeping that application in mind, we are able to keep several icons or windows open at one time. If we are not working with a particular file, we minimize them. The files are hidden from view but not closed. Those files could consist of anger, fear, jealousy, unforgiveness, idolatry, self-righteousness, addictions, and the list is long. If we continue to hide those issues or sins as they are, we are walking in darkness. We know God sees, but we foolishly believe the lies of the devil that no one can see our sins as we continue to hide, so we think!

Just like a computer, it will operate at a slower pace from a lot of open windows. If we do not close those windows of hidden sin (get deliverance), it will hinder our walk with God. If the system is shut down without closing those windows, the system will crash. If we do not deal with the sins in our hearts, there will be bad consequences to pay.

> Then He said to them, "Thus it is written, and thus it was necessary for the Christ to suffer and to rise from the dead the third day, and that repentance and remission of sins should be preached in His name to all nations, beginning at Jerusalem.
>
> Luke 24:46-47

Without repentance, there is no remission of sin. God will not open up your heart icon because He has given us free will. He will convict and only deliver us if we allow Him. Like the cat trying to hide in the dark, in order for me to come out of the darkness, I had to walk into the light. I had to come to terms with my own sins and strongholds. I realized it had to be less focused on my families' issues and more focused on mine.

Let no one deceive you with empty words,
for because of these things the wrath of God
comes upon the sons of disobedience.There-
fore do not be partakers with them. For you
were once darkness, but now you are light
in the Lord. Walk as children of light (for
the fruit of the Spirit is in all goodness, righteousness, and truth), finding out what is ac-
ceptable to the Lord. And have no fellowship
with the unfruitful works of darkness, but
rather expose them. For it is shameful even
to speak of those things which are done by
them in secret. But all things that are exposed
are made manifest by the light, for whatever
makes manifest is light. Therefore He says:
"Awake, you who sleep, arise from the dead,
and Christ will give you light."

Ephesians 5:6-14

My nephew changed an outside light over my garage
one time to a motion detector light. It would come on
once dark, but if anyone or critter came closer, a much
brighter light radiated the whole cul-de-sac. Nothing
was sneaking up close without being seen.

It's painful being exposed; we all try to hide our evil
thoughts, negative deeds, shameful mistakes. Think
about how much better life would be if we keep our

lights on, not allowing Satan to drag us back into darkness. I have running lights on my car that shine even in the daytime. No sneaking around in that car day or night. The brighter the lights, the less of the darkness. The more God exposed my darkness, the more I repented praying that the secret things of my heart come to light in order to receive my healing. The more I healed, the more beautiful my life bloomed.

My Roses

During the process of my healing, I became less obsessed with my search for the right family and pleasing people after realizing God has a sense of humor. After all, He created us all, right? Reflecting back on my life, God reminded me of a story I hold dear to my heart.

My stepdad came from a large family of eleven children. His father was a Church of God pastor from Michigan who organized many churches in the north, later to continue his ministry in Florida. I treasured all the times whenever the family got together for special occasions, with many of them sitting up late drinking coffee and reminiscing childhood stories. Dad would just laugh when I suggested he should document some of the family escapades. One of my favorite stories that would bring us all to tears with laughter repeated every year was about one of his sisters, named "Rosie."

The family often traveled having revivals, one being in a small country church out in the sticks, as we would say in the South. After the Sunday night service, they all loaded up in the car to head back home. Back then, there were no seatbelt laws or car seats for the little ones; we all just piled in the back seat. There were six of us kids, so I couldn't imagine how bad it was to travel with an even larger family. They arrived home late in the night only to discover as each child piled out of the car that Rosie was missing. With panic sinking in, his father raced back to the church with my dad and another one of his brothers.

This was a secluded church out in the woods, and everyone had gone. Keep in mind years ago, many country churches did not have an indoor restroom. But there was the old "outhouse" where, well, we just took care of business!

After searching the premises, they heard her crying and moaning in the "outhouse." She had fallen into the waste pit, and it was a miracle she was alive. You can imagine what she looked like and how she smelled when they pulled this terrified child out of all that mess. My Dad and brother just rolled with laughter being the boys they were. It didn't set too well with their father, and the boys didn't laugh very long. Later in life, as they relived that experience in laughter, it always ended with the comment, "that was the worst whipping they ever got!"

I recalled another story I read in my youth that is not humorous at all. This takes place in one of the Nazi concentration camps. It is heartbreaking to read of the death and torment the Jews were put through during that time. My mind still has a hard time comprehending such inhumane and torture.

The story told was about one of those survivors that had to work in the human waste pit day after day. The sight, smells, and bacteria alone at times were deadly. Somehow in all of that smelling waste, one beautiful lone rose grew up out of it. The sight of that perfect beautiful rose with its thorns restored his hope and faith, reminding him of the beauty of Christ in the middle of a mess.

Two stories here, each with a rose in the middle of human waste. The rose with thorny stems is the number one most beautiful flower with over one hundred species. Women love to get roses. It is often prized as a symbol of achievement, completion, and perfection.

As the Lord reminded me of these stories, I begin to recognize all the "roses" He has given me in my lifetime. They all have been beautiful roses that grew out of their own thorns, blooming in the middle of my messes. These roses were God-given in seasons of my own confusion and lack of self-worth, guiding me, supporting me, pushing me to the next level in God.

There are many, but I can only share with you the ones that impacted my life the most. I struggled with the fact if it would be appropriate to list their names because I did not want to hurt any feelings by leaving certain ones out. He reminded me that each rose has a species name and to give them the honor they deserve. With that, I feel it appropriate to name each of my roses.

These are my roses that God has given me:

Minnie Madaris—a Godly grandmother that help raise me, making my little clothes, praying many prayers over my life. She was a pillar of faith and stability.

An African American babysitter—she did not work for our family very long when I was a young child, so I can't remember her name. I never forgot the times she had me kneeling on my little knees beside her as she was prophesying and praying over me. I believe to this day she was breaking generational curses on my little life.

Neely Jeffords—my pastor's wife as a little girl at the Palace Street Church of God. I would sit on the front pew and watch her play that beautiful black grand piano leading the choir. Still very young and not play-ing yet, I would say to myself as a child, "one day, I am going to play that piano." Fifteen years later, I did play that grand and direct several of the choirs in that same church body for seven years.

Opal Bethume—she was my mom's BFF, whom she loved dearly. Opal was an excellent seamstress with such a sweet, giving heart, loyal to her family and friends. We were very poor and with three other siblings at that time, and my parents could not afford to buy new clothes. It seemed like Opal would make her daughter a new outfit every week. We were sometimes shocked if Cherry wore the same thing twice. I was always thrilled to see Opal coming in with a sack of clothes because we girls were about the same size. She kept me in style and was a blessing more than she knew.

Betty Jackson—another excellent seamstress I came to know around the age of eleven when we lived in Macon. By this time, I was interested in sewing. She was instrumental in teaching me sewing skills that I used the rest of my life. One thing about her I will never forget; if my seams were not straight, I had to rip them out and do it again. Till this day, I hate to rip out bad stitching, but she taught me to be excellent in what I did in every area of my life, and not half do anything.

Pastor Johnny Towns—Church of God pastor in Macon. I had not been playing the piano very long and only knew a few chords. I was twelve by this time when the church pianist left the church, and Pastor put me on the piano. As challenging as it was for all as you can imagine, we would somehow, with God's anointing, get through the song service. I grew in music as God blessed me for my efforts continuing to play there until we moved back to my hometown.

*Pastor Mark Summers—came to Palace Street later to build Central Lake Church of God, Griffin—*a godly man with a strong personality, and there was no playing around in his ministry. He taught me honesty, integrity, and never to water down God's word.

*Pastor Walter Pettit—Central Lake Church of God, Griffin—*he was one of my favorites. Quiet but very intelligent and one of the wisest, loving pastors I ever had. He gave me an opportunity to advance in our music program in not only playing the piano but also working with the choirs, never putting me in a religious box.

*Dr. James Lee—Digby Assembly of God—*this pastor came out of the Baptist movement into the Assemblies of God. Feeling he had new freedom in the church, he was a short firecracker for God. I have to say he was my most challenging pastor teaching me to dig out those nuggets in God's Word.

*Elizabeth Dunn—*a sweet, precious lady in our church I had known since a child. At a crossroads in my life, she was essential in helping me leave a dead-beat job behind, giving me an opportunity in a career that changed my life forever. She inspired me to get out of the boat and walk on water, not just in a spiritual sense but also in the natural.

The Skinner Family Singers—Terry, Gloria, Barbara Sue, Carolyn, David & Bruce. This family shared with me many victories, laughter, and heartaches as we ministered together in music for many years, along with my mother Mary, bass player Tommy Helton, Trombone-Bud Dunson, and guitarist Ricky Henson. David played the drums, and I was on the piano. They became my family, not just brothers and sisters in Christ but siblings from another mother. Once you had a Skinner in your ballpark, they were there for life.

Hugh Madaris—my father. I continue to honor him as my father for who he was, not in how we were raised. His blood runs through my veins. From him, I inherited his good traits and talents. My upbringing was bad at times, but God's grace made me the woman I am today.

Mary Agnes Hooker Sawyer—my beautiful mom and a blessing. She was precious, loving, and my sidekick. She bailed me out of more projects than I can name, supporting me in every way, allowing me to grow into the woman God had created. With a voice of an angel, I was privileged to minister in music alongside her until she was called to Heaven's choir.

John Wesley Sawyer—my godly stepdad. He taught me what a father should look like, loved me unconditionally, and in doing so, my perspective of my heavenly Father changed, helping me to understand how much God loved me. When God put my dad in my life, He gave me a bouquet of roses, not just one.

Lee Sullivan—my loving husband now in Heaven, my hero, with a lot of patience, taught me how to trust again, how to laugh and have fun in life, allowing me to take off my mask and be who God created me to be. Always with a giving heart showering me with flowers, gifts, and support in every way. He was my rose bush!

These are my closest friends old and new that I have allowed to speak into my life, many being like "sisters" from a different mother:

Sarah Thompson Taylor—has traveled this journey with me since the age of fourteen. We've shared many mountains and valleys together. She still encourages me to this day with a lot of laughs as we waddle through life together. Her love and support are endless!

Sharon Richardson Yarbrough—one of my spiritual sisters that have stood with me in the hard and trying times of life. Talented and unique, she speaks the truth to me in love, never being judgmental, and never wavering in her faith.

Sharon Hooks—another spiritual sister where her support and encouragement are unmeasurable. We too have walked through a lot of messes together, picking up roses along in our journey. We have sung, laughed, and cried together for many years.

Judy and Bill Christopher—Judy, now with our Father, was a "straight shooter." I can only imagine her playing the keys and helping with Heaven's choir. You knew exactly where you were in a relationship with her. Full of honesty and encouragement, praying for me often.

Bill—her loving husband, a spiritual brother, one of my favorite, humbled Bible teachers, full of integrity who inspired us all to dig deeper into God's word as he mentored us in ministry.

Rhonda Sample—a spiritual sister in Washington that I loved to sing, share and worship with. Her giftings are many, and I'll never be able to repay her for her support in my grief process. She was and still is available to pray with me, listen and let me cry.

Pam Pace—another sister in Washington that has been my female "Peter." She is like a rock, not afraid to tell it like it is. She has been my rock in my life, also encouraging and supporting me in the grief process. We often laugh and preach to each other!

Desiree Currington—a sister God dropped in my life in Washington. She was one of those "suddenly blessings" you hear about, being instrumental in helping me with a new business—Precious beyond words. In my struggle, she never gave up on me.

Pastor Victoria Bowen and Pastor Robynn Lynch—a mother and daughter team that stood by me in a very hard season of life, one on each side holding me up not only in prayer but in deeds as I dealt with the loss of Lee. They became family, being an inspiration, often showering me with flowers.

Brooke Baldasare Marin—a beautiful young lady that has been like a daughter for over fifteen years. Very loving, thoughtful, full of encouragement, direction, and a heart for God, always seeing the best in people. We've shared a lot of prayers and tears together in our journey. Everyone needs a 'Brooke' in their lives. This book would not have happened without her support. Special thanks and love to the Marin and Baldasare family's as they adopted me into their families.

Sandra Craig—a special and classy lady I met on one of my job that shared tears, hopes, and dreams during my journey. Her smiles, kindness, and support will never be forgotten.

Bobbie Addison—a precious sister that seemed to befriend me when no one else was around. One of the sweetest and giving hearts I know. She always has a smile even in the middle of her own storms, faithful to stand by her friends in the middle of theirs.

Glenda Landers—another sister in the Lord that worked with me. We often challenged each other in God's Word, her being Baptist and me Pentecostal with lots of laughs along the way. Our friendship has had no boundaries with denominations and has endured through the years.

Blake Madaris—my nephew who became my son. Who let me experience the joy and tears of parenthood when he was in my care. A tender and giving heart always available to help those in need.

Francis Bishop—an awesome spiritual sister that laughed, cried, and prayed with me for many years. Her faith, love, and supernatural incite have been inspiring.

I was never able to have children in the natural but God, through the years in different seasons of life, sent several spiritual sons and daughters I mentored and called mine, each one enriching my life: *Jeff and Felicia Baker, Carla Vega Gibson, Whitney Vega, Kim Taylor Brown, Candice Taylor Treadway, Rhonda Sharp Adams, Robynn Leach, Victoria Bowen, Jason Flores, Blake Madaris, Brooke, and Aaron Marin.*

My stepchildren—*Donna Hoyt, Erica Williams, and Sean Sullivan*—who, like their Dad has loved me unconditionally. These kid-lets, spouses, and children have been a blessing in my life, each one a rose of their own, and I won't let them go.

My siblings—*Doug, Shirley, Jane, Marvin, Wayne, and half-brother Tommy.* Our journeys have not always been on the same road, but I have been blessed through the years, having them in my life and having learned from each one. Together we have shared laughter, tears, and heartaches as we all struggle with our own issues of life. I would not trade them for any others.

All my nieces, nephews, cousins, in-laws, son/ daughters-in-law, and grandchildren are each a rose in my life, but too many to list.

Every one of my roses is unique, with names having their own identity and colors. Many of my roses have withered in the natural; gone home to be with the Lord. Their journey is finished here, but their beauty there is way beyond the beauty of a rose.

As the Lord helped me sort out my roses, I can't end this without naming the greatest and most beautiful perfect rose I've received of all. A color, fragrance, and majesty like none other. His name is *Jesus*!

In the book Song of Solomon 2:1-2, it reads, "I am the rose of Sharon, and the lily of the valleys. Like a lily among thorns, so is my love among the daughters."

This is a love chapter about the Shulamite woman being a bride and Solomon the bridegroom. Although it doesn't list Jesus, we conclude that Jesus is the Bridegroom in relationship with His church, the Bride, so we understand it would be Jesus coming to give us flowers or the giving of himself. He is the rose of Sharon.

We mustn't confuse the rose of Sharon with a rose with thorns. The rose of Sharon is native to south-central and southeast China but elsewhere, including much of Asia. The rose of Sharon is not part of the rose family but a hibiscus plant.

During Solomon's time, one of the largest valley plains in Palestine was a plain called Sharon that was considered to be wild, versatile, and was supposed to be known for the best and majesty in those days. So, I believe he was referring to a rose in the plain called Sharon.

Again, He said, "I" am the rose of Sharon. Of all the roses God has given me, Jesus tops them all. He is the "I am." The rose reminds me of how beautiful and perfect He is. He is perfect in love, just as the rose is the most perfect to all flowers in its beauty and smell.

My heart is like a vase that God has filled with beautiful roses, but if it wasn't for Jesus being *The Greatest Rose, the "I am"* that changed my heart, my vase would be empty.

Dad's little sister came out of her smelling, dark mess alive. The Jew in the story viewed a rose in the middle of his hellish mess, regaining hope and comfort as he was reminded Christ had not forgotten him or his situation. In the middle of my life messes, I learned to cling to the perfect rose of Sharon, Jesus Christ, as He pulled off the layers of band-aid's covering my wounds, changing my heart to be more like Him. It has been in those changes that I received more and more favor from God.

One Coat, Many Colors

I suppose if you were to sit down and have an honest discussion with your brothers and sisters, each one would have a different story of their growing up in life, regardless of what order they were in line. I've heard being the oldest child is hard, with the middle child even harder, with that one feeling overlooked. I can only speak, being the oldest from experience.

In relationships, there is always a pecking order, especially when more than one child is involved. Too often, we are caught up in fighting and criticizing each other, all needing attention and favor from our parents. Instead of taking responsibility for our own actions, we blame our siblings for things that go wrong in our young lives. We were masters of that game, good at blaming the other for what we did or tore up. That need for recognition grows into bitterness, jealousy, and resentment as we strive for significance.

I've learned what we really want is not so much to feel significant as to feel loved. Of course, the two are related. One reason why we have the need to be loved is because if loved by someone, we feel important to that person, friend, spouse, parent, or sibling. This love makes us feel significant. The difference in people is not so much what they want in love, as in the way they try to get what they want. If those needs are not met, we become very resentful of those we love.

One day a mother walked in to find her little daughter making ugly faces at the pet bulldog. When the mother scolded her, she answered: "well, he started it; look at him, I was just getting him back!"

Numerous times in my own family, we conveyed the same attitude being sure to get back at each other when our own expectations were not met. We certainly didn't live by Luke 6:27, 28 through thirty-six...

"But I say to you who hear: Love your enemies, do good to those who hate you, bless those who curse you, and pray for those who spitefully use you. To him who strikes you on the one cheek, offer the other also. And from him who takes away your cloak, do not withhold your tunic either. Give to everyone who asks of you. And from him who takes away your goods do not ask them back. And just

as you want men to do to you, you also do to
them likewise. "But if you love those who love
you, what credit is that to you? For even sinners love those who love them. And if you do
good to those who do good to you, what credit
is that to you? For even sinners do the same.
And if you lend to those from whom you hope
to receive back, what credit is that to you?
For even sinners lend to sinners to receive as
much back. But love your enemies, do good,
and lend, hoping for nothing in return; and
your reward will be great, and you will be
sons of the Most High. For He is kind to the
unthankful and evil. Therefore be merciful,
just as your Father also is merciful.

Luke 6:27-38

In reliving my childhood, there was a lot of bicker-
ing in our house, despitefully using each other for our
own gain with little respect for each other. Our love as
a family was far from what we had been taught in God's
Word. By not doing so, our resentment for each other
grew as we matured. Resentment is no stranger to any
of us and will become a pocket of poison in our hearts
if not dealt with.

My husband, in his late sixties, shared a story of an
incident repeatedly that happen in his childhood that

seemed to be burned into his memory so bad it remained there burning for many years. It was like "riding a dead horse," as some would say, one he could not get off. Him being the baby of four children, he was somewhat spoiled. Sometimes children seeing favoritism in their siblings will cause jealousy and resentment to manifest in their hearts, which are then acted on. This may be one reason this incident happened more than once. He could not forget the fear, feeling tormented as a toddler by his two middle siblings, who dragged him to the middle of the road, leaving him there screaming. The oldest sister would always rescue him.

It was a shame it took him years to confront them of his hidden hurt. They did not remember the incidents. As the years passed, his resentment grew toward them so much it actually was like cancer, that unknowing to them put a wedge in their relationships for a long time. When he released his resentment, after a lot of prayers, he was able to confront them, forgave them, and able to have a relationship that had been tainted for many years.

The Bible is full of illustrations of Sybil rivalry, but I want to focus on a story in the book of Genesis beginning at verse 35:12 , God said, "The land which I gave Abraham, and I give to you; and to your descendants, after you, I give this land."

Abraham was the father of Isaac; Jacob, the son of Isaac. God gave Jacob the same promise He gave his grandfather. The land will also be yours. We know later God changed Jacob's name to Israel in 35:10. He had six sons by Leah; Reuben, Simeon, Levi, Juda, Issachar, and Zebulun; two by Leah's maidservant; Gad and Asher. His favorite wife, Rachel's maidservant, bore Dan and Naphtali, with Rachel bearing her two sons Joseph and Benjamin. This was the beginning of the twelve Tribes of Israel. Joseph was born to Rachel in her old age but died in childbirth having Benjamin.

It was not a hidden fact that Jacob not only loved Joseph more than his other 11 sons and numerous daughters but demonstrated a lot of favoritism toward him. I can only imagine the trials and tribulations of raising several children on a daily basis, with each one striving for recognition from their parents. It can be hard not to have a favorite.

The story goes that because Jacob favored Joseph more than the other children, he made him a tunic, or we define it as a coat, of many colors. The Bible tells us Jacob made it. I thought maybe he had one of the ladies make it, but that's not what we read, and I assume it was sewn together.

Being a seamstress for many years myself, I know there is a process in making a garment. You have to first come up with an idea, measure, make a pattern, choose the fabric then assemble it. Not a fast process for sure. As with any seamstress in creating a garment, there is a lot of love and a feeling of accomplishment in each finished product. Jacob had to be pleased and gratified from his creation of the coat of love he had made for his precious son.

I try to picture in my own mind how the fabrics were put together, what kind of cloth and colors were sewn together. Were there strips up or down, any circles, or mismatched designs? We know it was very colorful and beautiful because it was easy to see him walking from a distance. There is no doubt in my mind Joseph had to notice how special he was to his father and, just maybe, had developed an arrogant, prideful attitude toward his family.

By the age of seventeen, Joseph had become quite a thorn in his brothers' lives. At times he told on his brothers for things that were not pleasing to Jacob. I hated when my siblings told on me. No one likes a tattletale. An older child can understand for a little while why the parents shelter the little ones, but if it continues as they mature, the older ones begin to feel not loved as much and resentful. Too often, I would tell my own mother that I couldn't believe she let my younger siblings get by with things that I was punished for.

His brothers hated him for a long time, never speaking any words of encouragement or try to mentor him.

To make matters worse, as God gave Joseph prophetic dreams, the family seem to feel Joseph was bragging about revealing those dreams, as their resentment and hatred toward him increased. Jacob had to know how much the boys envied Joseph, but he overlooked it, instead continued displaying more favoritism by making Joseph a special coat, one of a kind.

As the story continues, the brothers went out to feed the flock in Shechem. Their dad decided to send Joseph to Shechem to check on their progress. After reaching Shechem, Joseph finds out they had actually moved the herd to Dothan, so he takes off in that direction. Joseph had tattled on them before, and here he is again spying on them, so they may have felt. The brothers recognize him coming from a long distance wearing his colorful coat and begin mocking him, calling him names, a "dreamer" for one.

Their hate was so strong at this point they conspired to kill him. His brother Rueben tried to discourage the others from murder by suggesting they put him in a pit close by instead of killing him, with the intentions of slipping back later to rescue him, but while he was away from the camp, a caravan came along, and they sold Joseph to some Midianite traders.

The brothers returned home with Joseph's tunic covered with animal blood asking their dad if it was Joseph's. Such deception, hate, and resentment from his brothers had manifested. The sad thing was Jacob just assumed a wild animal had killed him and never questioned them. Satan still uses the same device today; he does not give us the truth, just influences us to believe a lie!

We know of the many trials and temptations Joseph went through as his dreams were unfolded over several years. It is interesting to see how children's character takes shape when one has been spoiled, set aside, and favored above others. Is it possible that he had developed a sense of pride and superiority from his dreams as he revealed those dreams to his family? Maybe he had to go through his trials and humbling seasons of lies, betrayal, and being forgotten before God raised him to power as the second in charge to rule over Egypt.

To fast forward the story as God unfolded Joseph's dreams, the Egyptian Pharaoh put Joseph in charge of the food supply. Many came from miles around to buy food, including his brothers. They did not recognize him as they stood before this powerful man God had raised up from out of a pit that they personally threw him in. Joseph had the power to put them to death, but instead, in his humility, he hid alone and welp, still loving them regardless of how they had treated him. He rose above any resentment and hate he could have had against his brothers.

As I pondered on this story, my heart went out to all the brothers and sisters that have been mistreated and abused by their siblings, for whatever reason. I now understand how my siblings became distant toward me, feeling our parents favored me over them.

What they did not understand is how unique and special they were. They constantly fought with each other, trying to feel better about themselves and resenting me. At times their struggles with jealousy, envy, low self-esteem, and resentment made life hard for us all.

Joseph's brothers struggle with the same issues feeling somewhat they were not as important and as loved as Joseph. It was sad that Jacob did not deal with his issues in showing favoritism, and it is sad parents thru the ages have practiced the same behavior, not realizing the damaging effects on the other children. Because Joseph's brothers did not deal with their resentment, it soon developed into hate. Unfortunately, children still fight family favoritism today!

One coat had been made by a father who loved his favorite son. A coat of many colors, shapes, and pattern sizes, one well planned out with the best materials in mind. If we could only understand that God, our heavenly Father, has made in each one of us a coat of many colors, talents, and giftings, more than we can comprehend. Psalm 139:14 reads, "I will praise You, for I am fearfully and wonderfully made; marvelous are Your works, and that my soul knows very well." We must know who we are in Christ and how special and different we are to Him.

Through the years, God has revealed many different colors of my life while watching the many colors of talents and giftings become brighter in my brothers' and sisters' lives. Each one of them is a beautiful coat, each different in their giftings and talents.

Once we believe and know who we are in Christ, we will recognize that God loves us all the same, no favoritism, each one of us as a special coat, each one created differently in His image. When we declare we will no longer live in resentment and hate of our siblings, regardless of how much favoritism there may be in our family, we begin to live in love, peace, and acceptance of each other. He gives us all dreams and visions, but we must not be envious of others we've encountered, especially our family. I pray we begin to see ourselves through His eyes and recognize the person He has created each one of us to be. Because of the Father's love, He created each one of us like that one special coat but each one with many beautiful colors.

A Preacher's Kid with God's Favor

As our own family circus was spinning out of control, additional pressures were added along with the label known as *Preacher's Kid*. One day hopefully, the church will understand that Children of pastors do not have to be perfect examples for all the other children in the church. They are not any different and do not have a different set of rules. No child should carry that cross. Whenever a pastor with children or staff leaders in a church does not allow Holy Spirit to deal with the hearts of their children, trying to force perfection and salvation on them will be dangerous. It drives them away from the cross, not to it.

This type of stress will cause many PKs to slip around in rebellion, hiding their actions. Have you ever heard people say that the PKs are the worst with the joke that it's because they hang around with the members' kids? Often when the pastor father finds out the mistakes of their child, they try to hide it for fear the news will tarnish their Ministry, which can create secrets of their own. We have to be held accountable for our actions regardless of our titles. Not all pastors are guilty, realizing they have to allow their children to learn and grow, knowing they can't fix, control, or save them. If the church loved the PKs unconditionally, with more pastors mentoring their children instead of controlling, I think less would walk away from their faith.

Carrying the added burden of needing to be a perfect PK drove me deeper into my own fantasies of what I thought a Christian family should look like. Giving up somewhat on having a different family, I married in hopes of making my own perfect little family. The statement is true that if you don't deal with your own issues, you will carry them over into other relationships. And yes, I packed all of mine in several boxes, carried over into other relationships.

Most flaws in my relationship with my family were because my expectations ran high and very judgmental. While I strived to be perfect, I felt my family should also, therefore living most of my life disappointed. To add to my people-pleasing tenancy's I was also labeled bossy and a fixer. In my heart, I believed as a mature, responsible Christian girl; it was my duty to fix everyone in my family, including my husband.

I wasted years of trying to fit him into my "ideal perfect husband mold." Instead of allowing God to change him, I tried to help God, driving my unmet expectations of him deeper, causing him to be more miserable as the years passed, which destroyed our relationship. As with my siblings, so with my husband, *I was not emotionally present and available unless it was on my terms.* I continued in my workaholic lifestyle only to numb my feelings of pain, more than ever convincing myself I would never be good enough for him, regardless of the home I had, how high I climb the corporate ladder, or what kind of ministry I was involved in.

After my divorce, I thought life would be more peaceful with a fresh start by moving away from my hometown. There was a freedom of not having to be accountable to everyone I ran into on the streets from living in a small town. After my move, it didn't take long to realize it wasn't the church I attended, family, friends, or my town. The problem was with me. I had believed the lies of the devil that I was damaged goods since the beginning of my teens. My childhood dream of being a minister's wife was shattered. Like my father, in my own way, I was hiding under a pile of excuses, blaming my family for not meeting my expectations.

Thru the years, I was blessed to have several new homes thinking that would fill some of the voids in my life. I liked to paint, design, and make it my own. There is a lot of planning to coordinate the right color scheme, layout, and placement of the furniture in each room. It would normally start off fresh and clean with every item in its place, but it didn't take long that I started to hide unused items in the closets with an overflow into a designated room.

We all have that one room or the garage that catches everything until it is so full you can barely walk through it. That space is no longer used for what it was intended for. I don't know why we hang on to stuff as we do. In our minds, we think we will be able to use it again one day. Sometimes we do, but more times than not, we just collect it, hid in locked rooms where we are too ashamed to let anyone see our mess. In my journey, I found junked-up rooms in my heart. The more I prayed that God would search and cleanse my heart, the more doors He unlocked, showing me my ugly mess.

That was some of my father's downfall. He locked the doors of his heart, not allowing God to free him fully. From watching his life, I determined to not fall into the same pattern as he; to be accountable for my sins, stay the course in my faith and relationship with God. The more I sincerely sought Him, the more I had to deal with my own heart issues I was hiding behind.

It was a hard statement from my sister but made me face the truth when she said that I was ashamed of our family, the one God had given me, and also how He created me. By my father's words, he was also ashamed, being that his mother was a poor widow woman, and because of that, he didn't have a chance in life. I had to grieve God's heart with my years of questioning His creation of me as I complained about the "blessings" of the family He has given me.

Some months back, I had written a short story named My Roses for another project but felt the Lord wanted me to include it in this book. In my original list of roses, I did not include my father. While editing this book, I heard the Holy Spirit say, "if you truly honor your father, you will include him as a rose." The roses in the previous chapter were people that had made an impact in my life, the reason for honoring them. So did my father in a different sense. Many thorns grow in the stem of a beautiful rose. Every one of my roses, in the natural sense, has their thorns, including my father, but because of God's grace, most were able to go around the thorns they were encountered with.

Because my father did not maneuver around his thorns very well, he was not able to live his life victoriously. Although he grew up in a Christian home, he developed a victim mentality. Proverbs 23:7 reads, "for as he thinks in his heart, so is he." He believed the lies of Satan more than the truths of God's word about who "he" was in Christ. It took a lifetime, but at the end of his life, he finally got it.

Doctors can quickly diagnose some problems while others may have to go through a series of tests, and they can be somewhat painful. In a painful test of the spirit, my healing took a long time because I believed lies from satan, continuing years before I allowed God to diagnose my problem. God knew all along, but I would not allow Him to make that transformation in my life. It was only when I recognized my strongholds and *let go of my need to know* about family secrets, God was able to do healing in my life.

Over many years as I watched the Christian families I envied for so long fall apart, secrets in their own lives unveiled, many were a lot worse than mine. The more horror stories revealed, the more I appreciated the family I had wanted to trade for so long.

Finally, I came to peace that I was in the family God designed for me. Not all Christian homes are as dysfunctional as mine was; some are much worse. There are no guarantees the parents or the children will be everything we desire as a family unit. In our family circus, we all have issues, some more or less, some more ugly than others.

I dealt with a lot of guilt coming to a conclusion; if I hadn't been so concerned with myself, perhaps I could have been a stronger influence in the lives of my siblings. Life is not about who is right or wrong, but it's realizing regardless of the road each family member travels, they are God-given roses. It's about allowing God to change us, by faith believing regardless of how hard our life becomes. "He who began a new work in you is faithful to complete it" (Philippians 1:6).

Later in life, I was blessed to remarry and move to the beautiful Pacific Northwest. Even after living there for many years, I continued to marvel at God's creation, saying often, people here do not appreciate what they are looking at, with the rolling mountains sometimes revealing snowcaps; the stunning volcanoes erecting high in their majesty; the beautiful waters of Puget Sound full of God's creatures.

In the awesomeness of all that beauty, we fail to forget that there is no traction without friction. The rolling of the mountains over time has developed because of the shifting and friction of the tectonic plates pushing the mountains higher and higher. The earth groans as the plates shift. The strains and friction in our lives are never pleasant. Like the beautiful Pudget Sound, there will be no development or beauty in our lives if we run, trying to stop the friction as painful as it can be at times. But if we go through the process, the end results will be breathtaking.

In all of David's running, battles, and hiding, he found that secret place in God. He wrote this song of praise when he fled from Saul in the cave.

My heart is steadfast, O God, my heart is steadfast; I will sing and give praise. Awake, my glory! Awake, lute and harp! I will awaken the dawn. I will praise You, O Lord, among the peoples; I will sing to You among the nations. For Your mercy reaches unto the heavens, and Your truth unto the clouds. Be exalted, O God, above the heavens; let Your glory be above all the earth.

Psalm 57:7-11

I must keep my heart fixed on the Lord, giving Him thanks in all His blessings no matter how many thorns I have to maneuver around. My family is dear to me now more than ever before, each a beautiful rose learning how to maneuver around their own thorns. Who am I to try and change who God created them to be?

I no longer question Him for answers; they were there all the time. As God healed me in time, He also healed our relationships. I love them all from the bottom of my heart as I deeply say I wouldn't trade the family God gave me with anyone. I am truly blessed with God's favor, one so undeserved!

So, when you catch yourself not liking your family, just take a long look around. You will find some worse than yours. Don't be ashamed or complain about them, but pray and be thankful for where God put you as He molds your character to become the man and woman after His own heart!

Notes

New King James — Thomas Nelson Publishers

The Amplified Bible — Zondervan Publishing House

Family Circus — Wikipedia